susan p. meisel & ellen harris

HAMPTONS
pleasures

photography by susan p. meisel

HARRY N. ABRAMS, INC., PUBLISHERS

CONTENTS

6 introduction

8 map

12 getting here

29 being here

60 tastes of summer

78 dining alfresco

87 take the plunge

104 in the gardens

123 no better than this

132 home sweet home

163 endnote

164 glossary of place names

166 acknowledgments

introduction

WE MET MORE THAN A DOZEN YEARS AGO, thrown together quite by accident in a tennis game. We were two lefties with an undeniable passion for the beach. After an exhilarating 11–9 score, we sat down to cool off and couldn't stop talking for hours. Our love of the Hamptons was the first common thread between us, but we quickly discovered a long list of similar interests. We both grew up spending our summers at different seashores, but our love for the beach eventually brought us together in the Hamptons, this magical stretch of easternmost Long Island where so much of our time over the last twenty-five years has been spent. For both of us, the love affair with the Hamptons began slowly, taking place only on summer weekends, but soon intensifying to weekends throughout the year, and then holidays were added, until finally we just couldn't get enough of it! ★ We like to tell everyone that Exit 70 on the Long Island Expressway is the road to paradise. The Hamptons are a mix of country and beach, a delightful change of pace from the city, a place to idle away

the hours, taking time out for yourself, your family, your friends. But it becomes real only when you start to smell the salt air and feel your sanity return. ✶ This is our second book about the Hamptons. After the first, *The Hamptons: Life Behind the Hedges,* we found we couldn't stop the looking, the exploring of hidden places, the process of capturing its beauty on film. As more and more rolls were developed it became clear that we had enough for yet another book. Our deep, abiding passion for this place overflows from the first book into this one. This is our insider's view of the pleasures of the Hamptons: Here we have more houses, gardens, privets, pools, more of everything to show you. The remarkable beauty of this countryside is inspiring—its beaches, big sky, fields, ocean—like so many before us and the many that will follow, we've fallen under its spell and been utterly taken in by its charms. We hope you will be too by the time you've reached the end of this book, our tribute to our favorite place on earth, the Hamptons.

the hamptons
LONG ISLAND, N.Y.

KICK BACK AND RELAX, THE WEEKEND IS ALMOST HERE! On Wednesday, television clicker in hand, the search is on for the weather report. Everyone says that weather doesn't matter, but of course it does. There are so many questions, like what to do first when you get out here . . . the choice is yours. Whether you are a homeowner, renter, or guest, transportation is the first issue. Come by car, bus, or train, or throw your paycheck to the wind and book a helicopter or small plane. Once here, the prescription for a great weekend is so varied it's overwhelming—it might include fresh-baked muffins after a morning jog, lounging poolside with a good book, sandwiches on the beach, a late afternoon bike ride, homemade ice-cream, a nap, or an invitation to a BBQ down the road. A few friends invited over for dinner turns into a dozen or more, so make a new rule: Guests of guests cannot bring a guest even if they're a superstar! Granted, it can be hard

getting here

work fitting it all in, but the pay-off is huge, and, fortunately, doing absolutely nothing is an option. ✷ Southampton first became a summer destination for wealthy New Yorkers back in the late 1800s when it was the last stop on the train. Farming was very much the way of life back then, but this environment suited those seeking an escape from the fast pace and heat of the city. As the Long Island Railroad was extended further east, the other quaint towns of the East End (the Hamptons area of Long Island) became accessible. Soon the city folk who came out here were looking for more than just a weekend getaway, and since, being the upper class, staying in other people's homes or local inns wasn't too appealing, they built their own residences. Designed on a grand scale, these elaborate, shingle-clad "cottages," as they were called then, were nothing less than magnificent mansions surrounded by wide lawns and lush gardens. Artists, hearing rhapsodies about the Hamptons' quiet natural beauty and the unusual luminosity of its light, soon followed and eventually formed one of the most famous artist colonies in the country. By the early twentieth century word had traveled, and people from all walks of life started coming out to find their favorite spot in this farming community by the sea.

On the way to Sag Harbor

WE USED TO BE SUMMER PEOPLE, NOW WE COME OUT ALL YEAR-ROUND, and the reasons are clear. In the city you become bogged down with a million things to do, deadlines to meet, obligations to carry out, parties to attend, all causing stress and tension as you try to squeeze everything into a meager 24 hours each day. Typically, it's a hectic, fast-paced lifestyle, one that can wear you out and distract you from the important things in life. Being out in the Hamptons—the Hamptons that we know and love—brings you back down to earth, back down to what's real. Life is simpler here: the air is cleaner, the food tastes better, and the

being here

assault on the senses that you get in the city is completely gone. It's soothing and calming here, and the quiet allows you to stop, take a deep breath, and take a fresh, new look at life. ✳ The sea-bleached shingles on the old farm houses, the uncomplicated architecture, the light, sky, water, flat landscape, and the best soil for growing makes farmers of us all. The Hamptons—the string of towns from Southampton to Montauk to Shelter Island—used to be all about farming and fishing. We do not have all those open spaces anymore, too many houses have been built, but there are still enough working farms out here that it is not an uncommon sight to see a farmer on his red tractor preparing the fields. Actually, it's a most pleasant sight, for it's a harbinger of the sweet corn, fresh-dug potatoes, and sun-ripened tomatoes to come, and the color palette of those ever-changing fields is unforgettable.

Sagaponack

THE TINY HAMLETS AND VILLAGES OF THE HAMPTONS
are connected by borders of hedgerows, kettle ponds,
and the endless sea, making it hard to distinguish where
one begins and the other ends. Lined up like pearls
on a string (aka Montauk Highway), Southampton is
the first pearl on the strand, where old mansions
embrace the shoreline, reminding us of the wealth of
years gone by when seaside vacations first became
chic. It was here where the elite first began summering,
attracted by the broad white beaches and the proximity
to Manhattan, only seventy-five miles away. Private
railroad cars arrived carrying entire families coming
to stay for the whole summer. The children, their gov-
ernesses, maids in starched uniforms, and even the
family dog all enjoyed living by the sea. Southampton
today still retains a distinct aura of wealth and privacy
with its long driveways and high hedges shielding
the houses from view.

Now, on to the next pearl on the strand, the little
known hamlet of Water Mill, which takes its name
from a water mill built in 1644. Water Mill has a more
subtle ambience than Southampton. Blink your eyes
and you hardly know you've been there except for the
traffic, which has forced people to scout out different
routes. We have taken many a bike ride to June and
the late Harvey Morris's candy store in the middle
of town to get our favorite licorice (it was Harvey's
favorite too!). From here you can see all of Mecox Bay
out to the Atlantic Ocean. The people who make Water
Mill their home take pride in the fact that they have
managed to keep one of the most charming areas of
the Hamptons a well-guarded secret. On your way out
of Water Mill stop at Peachie and Ray Halsey's Organic
Green Thumb farm stand. These fruits and vegetables
have been gathered from land owned by twelve
generations of Halseys.

East Hampton

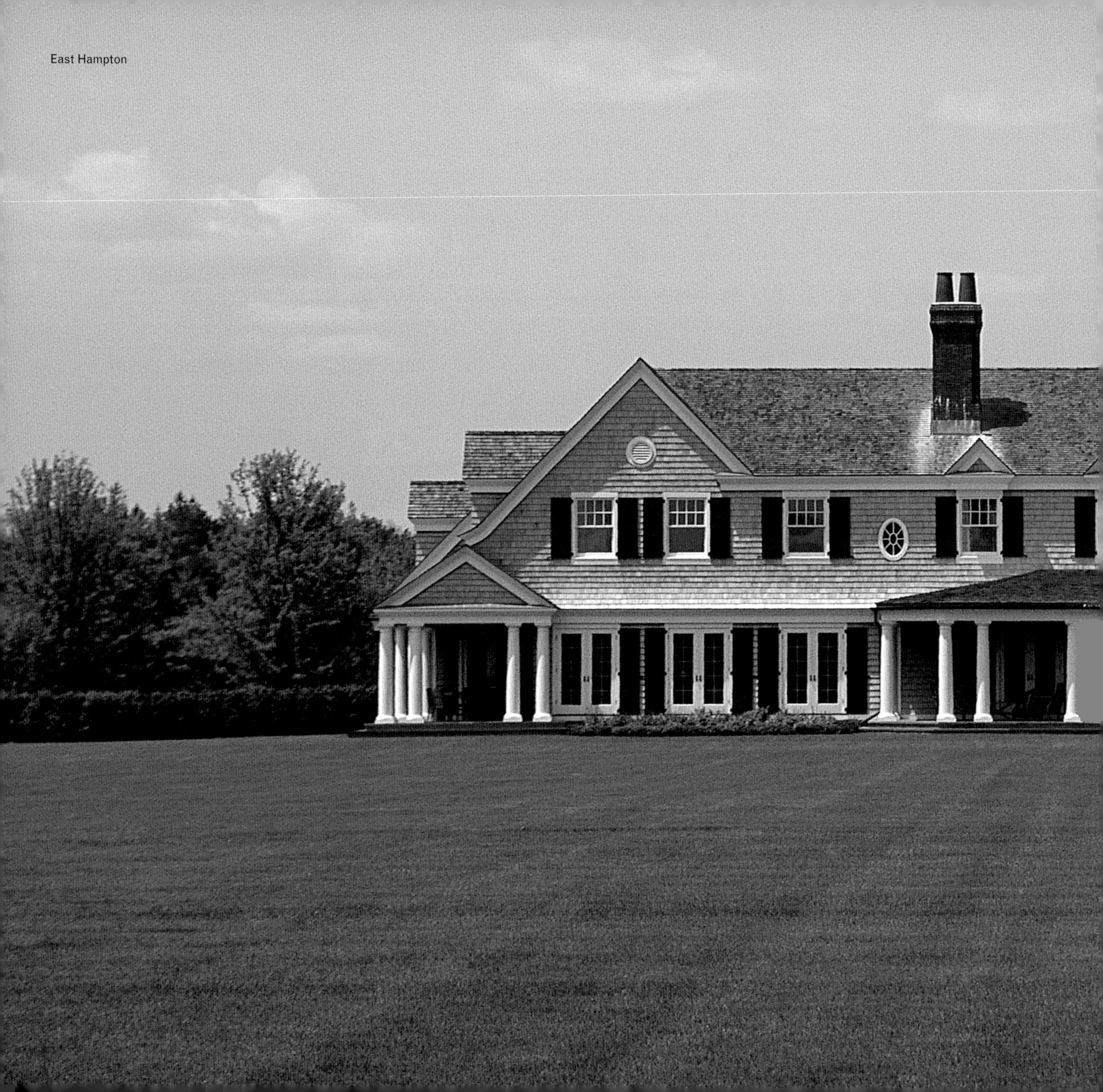

THE FARMING COMMUNITY OF BRIDGEHAMPTON IS NEXT on our string of pearls, with soil so rich it can grow just about anything, and Ocean Road, whose destination is obvious. The Candy Kitchen is a well-known, old-fashioned luncheonette where children are weaned on homemade ice cream. Local legend has it that one morning a man was found sitting at the counter in his bathrobe, mug in hand, thinking he was at home! This place is a must for the best BLT sandwiches east of New York.

Cross the little bridge of Sagg Pond, and you have arrived at a jewel of a place. Sagaponack, with its endless white-sand beaches, working farms, big sky, and rich soil, is our favorite place on earth. Sagaponack's downtown consists of a house, the original front door of which is now in the back and the back door is now in the front. The post office shares half of the house with the general store. Town meetings are held here as well, but bring your own beach chair and be prepared to rub shoulders with the likes of Kurt Vonnegut, Peter Matthiessen, Roy Scheider, Ross Bleckner, Stephanie Seymour, and the local farmers whose families have been here for generations.

Wainscott, the westernmost part of East Hampton township, borders on Georgica Pond. The approach to East Hampton village is made memorable by the sight of Town Pond where several generations of swans make their home. Although many of the stores in town are now owned by big-name designers, the town still retains its quaint charm. East Hampton has more than its share of streets—Further, Middle, and Hither to name a few—lined with gorgeous homes and gardens, all of which take you to the ocean.

A drive down Lily Pond Lane reveals old shingled mansions, sumptuous manicured gardens, famous inhabitants (most of the time you can't see them, of course), and memorable vistas.

Bridge Lane, Sagg Pond

Town Pond, East Hampton

THE NEXT PEARL ON THE MONTAUK HIGHWAY IS Amagansett, a village the Indians once referred to as "the place of good fishing." You can spend the day here at Asparagus Beach, the famous '70s hangout that derives its name from the fact that people spend far more time standing (like so many stalks of asparagus) and socializing than lying down.

And finally there's Montauk, a fisherman's nirvana, the easternmost tip on the island. Some say you can even see Portugal on a clear day.

Now backtrack a bit. If you travel north from Bridgehampton or Sagaponack you'll come to Sag Harbor, the once sleepy whaling town, dating back to the 1600s. In Sag Harbor, where a perfect balance is struck between old and new, historic houses and buildings, lovingly restored, share the same block with restaurants serving the latest trends in cuisine.

The hidden hamlet of North Haven is just beyond the Sag Harbor bridge. If you are fortunate enough to know someone with a boat, a ride on Great Peconic Bay is worth the views of magnificent tucked-away homes.

Now, a five-minute ferry ride will take you to a beautiful, remote oasis called Shelter Island. The island derives its name from the fact that it is located between two fingers of land, called the North and South Forks, thus it is sheltered by the forks of Long Island. It's worth spending a day here driving or biking through the rolling hills, taking in the Victorian architecture, stone walls, and hidden drives. There's a definite 1950s feel here, as if all the clocks had been turned back in this sleepy backwater where many of the 1950s-era shops and restaurants are still bustling.

ALL WINTER LONG WE DRIVE PAST JIM AND JENNIFER PIKE'S EMPTY STAND on Sagg Main in Sagaponack waiting for the wagons to fill up with the bounty from summer fields. It's been such a long wait!! Although the winter of 2002–03 was one of the worst on record, Pike's stand finally opened with huge red and yellow peppers, leeks, bib lettuce, red lettuce, beets, corn, sugar snap peas, and tiny orange tomatoes. You need to buy several boxes of these little tomatoes because we guarantee they'll be gone by the time you get home—they're so delectable it's impossible to resist popping them into your mouth like candy kisses, one after the other. One of the rituals of summer in the Hamptons has begun. ✳ A conversation at dinner may start with how awful the traffic was and how long it took to get here but it invariably turns to which stand has the best corn, best tomatoes, best potatoes. Everyone believes they know where to find the best, but the truth is you can't really go wrong no matter where you are. Everything is picked daily, at the moment of ripest perfection, and there is no match for fresh fruit right off the vine. By the end of July a fruit salad is a bike

tastes of summer

ride away and by the end of August the bounty is so full you need a car! Corn from the fields of Sagaponack taste like sugar and Long Island potatoes are true to their reputation—they're so good you can pull one out of the ground, clean it off, and eat it then and there like an apple. Tomatoes still warm from the field, thin skinned and juicy, are like nothing else you've tasted. Yellow and white peaches are piled high in old wooden crates, and old-fashioned green cardboard boxes are lined up in neat rows and filled with blackberries, blueberries, and strawberries—a pie-in-the-making! Have you ever tried Brussels sprouts just off the stalk? The full, nutty flavor is heavenly. Asparagus, nurtured by the salt air and seasonal rains (and seaweed covered beds to ensure a good-sized stalk), is ready in the spring; corn and tomatoes start showing up at local stands in July; the end of July is the beginning of potato season; and broccoli the size of bridal bouquets start appearing around August.

UPON YOUR RETURN TO THE CITY (IF YOU MUST!), THE BEST gift is a brown sack filled with an assortment of Hamptons-grown fruits and vegetables. Those city folk not lucky enough to receive a bag of these precious gems turn green with envy!

Marilee Foster grew up on a farm in Sagaponack just a short walk from the beach. Her family has been farming out here for generations, but it was Marilee who first established a farm stand. The first one was not much larger than a child's lemonade stand, but it grew to become a well-known stop for those in search of the freshest produce, and it's worth a trip just to see her hand-colored vegetable signs. She has a huge variety of crops. Have you ever eaten a white tomato, a green tomato with a blush of red, or even a purple-almost-black tomato? Here you'll have the chance to try these and many more. Her spring asparagus are without equal, and once you've had her heirloom tomatoes it's hard to pass her stand without stopping. Twenty-five years ago most of the stands were self-serve. You brown-bagged what you wanted and put your money in a coffee can. Marilee has kept that tradition alive—it's like tallying your own score during a game of golf.

On the backroads of Wainscott, Lisa and Bill's is another favorite stand. Ceci (Lisa and Bill's mother) minds her tractor-driven farm stand that had its beginnings as a means to raise college funds for her children. It started at the end of her driveway with the surplus from the adjacent fields. She subsequently moved to a more choice location on Wainscott Main. Her yellow and white corn is her specialty, and here's a tip: They have a small fridge filled with fresh mozzarella just waiting for tomato and basil.

The salt air of the Hamptons builds an appetite, which, luckily for us, is easily satisfied by these tastes of summer and the hard work of our local farmers.

Sagaponack

Sagaponack

IN THE EARLY MORNING fog rolls in over the fields forming a wet mist, but the rising sun and a welcoming ocean breeze will eventually burn it off. Time seems to stand still out here.

DINNER IN THE HAMPTONS IS FAR LESS COMPLICATED THAN IN THE CITY. The simple way we cook when we are here is what

it's all about. The ingredients are fresh and full of their own natural flavors, requiring little in the way of seasoning and

preparation. All you need to do is get a pot of water boiling, add some local steamers followed by some lobsters, toss a

fresh salad, add some just-picked corn from the stand down the road, and top it all off with a colorful medley of berries

for dessert. Now add the beach with its salty sea air, which seems to enhance the flavor of nearly everything, and you

have the recipe for a memorable summer dinner. ✱ As the sun sets behind the dunes, many take advantage of another

type of dining experience: On beautiful evenings cars are scattered helter-skelter on the beach and good food, cold

drinks, and convivial conversation flow freely. And it is not uncommon to see families arriving on the beach on foot, grill

in hand, coolers filled with the evening fare, and Capricorn

dining alfresco

and Orion as guests. On a clear night, the skies become so

filled with stars it's like dining in a planetarium. ✱ Fresh

blue fish is a must when you're by the sea. Groups of seagulls

hovering over the water signal the arrival of schools of blues, and suddenly there is a feeding frenzy as they dive-bomb

the water. Back on shore, eager fishermen quickly cast their lines. Sometimes the gulls will start to move down the beach

in pursuit of a shifting school, and it's hilarious to watch the fishermen yank their lines in, grab their rods, and start run-

ning to catch those fish. Lines are recast . . . dinner is about to appear. . . . success! Toss that blue on the grill, then add

a squeeze of lemon, a splash of olive oil, and the best fish you ever tasted is served. Now open a bottle of chilled local

wine and enjoy! ✱ Taking your meals poolside is yet another pleasure of summer. The barbecue is red hot, the table is

beautifully set, flowers from the garden are freshly cut, someone has just lit the candles, and dinner is about to begin.

It is a moment repeated so many times during the summer that the memories are kept alive all year long.

POOLS ARE EVERYWHERE IN THE HAMPTONS. For so many it's a necessary part of summer, an extension of the house, practically an outdoor living room. It's the place to be on a hot day cooling off, splashing about, quietly contemplating the world, or pretending you're Esther Williams. Laps are just the right exercise for those who don't want to get involved in endless summer activities. A swim under a star-studded moonlit sky can be very romantic. A rumor circulated for a while that someone had actually frozen their pool for ice-skating. ✳ The pool is often the focal point of the garden. On a recent tour of garden pools, we realized how important their placement is in the scheme of things, how vital their design to the overall impact of the garden. The color of a pool can change the mood—turquoise-blue can conjure up images of Mexico or the Caribbean, whereas a navy-blue pool can take you back to that dark lake at summer camp. A pool can pro-

take the plunge

vide the backdrop for a wide variety of theater or it can create an atmosphere that is soothing and serene. Forty-foot cedars form a dramatic curtain around one pool we visited, making it feel like a stage set. At another pool, a perfectly trimmed lawn, like a lush carpet of emerald green, runs right up to the edge of the pool itself. Another pool we visited on a pond in Sag Harbor is not your typical blue rectangle: Boulders and rocks set in and around the edge make it look more like a natural-occurring body of water somewhere up in the mountains than a pool, there is very little lawn to speak of, the sky is hidden by trees, and the play of dappled sunlight creates a dreamy atmosphere. ✳ The pool is a great place for owners to show off their green thumb. Poolside gardens may feature pergolas dripping with roses, wisteria-hung trellises, or pots overflowing with cascading summer blooms. Naturally, all of this creates a place for reading, relaxing, and entertaining. Floating on a raft allows the sensation of being part of the landscape—eye level with the grass, you can lazily watch it grow if you like. Best of all, a pool gives you the feeling of being in the lap of luxury.

BELOW: North Haven   OPPOSITE: Lily Pond Lane, East Hampton

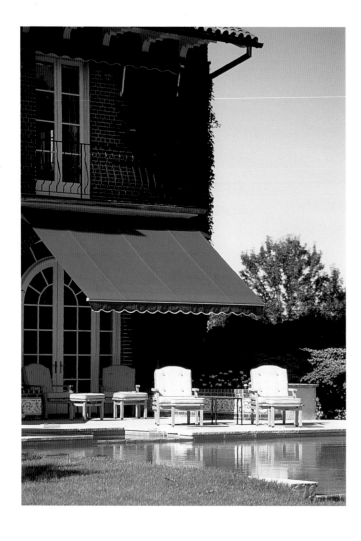

A FAVORITE PASTIME OF OURS IS A DAY-LONG BIKE RIDE, stopping here and there as our fancy takes us to explore other people's gardens. In the village of Sag Harbor, where the houses are so close together there's little room to spare, people manage quite well with what they have. Here a garden begins at the front gate by the sidewalk and meanders, never straying far, along the path to the front door. These exquisite cottage gardens are as practical as they are ornamental: roses ramble among cabbages, snap peas share the trellis with clematis, and honeysuckle, day lilies, hollyhocks, and hydrangeas share the soil with onions, cucumbers, leeks, and tomatoes. ✳ As we bike off toward the beach, quaint streets give way to wider avenues where sumptuous estate houses rise above perfectly manicured hedges. It's a challenge to catch a glimpse of the formal gardens behind these thick green walls! Century-old beech trees stand guard

in the gardens

over cutting gardens where you might spy the owner, clippers in hand, sun hat on, holding a basket of fresh-cut perennials. There is a house in Bridgehampton where the garden came before the house: the owners simply couldn't wait, and while the house was still a blueprint, the garden was completed. All four sides of the property were planted with roses entwining fences, and perennials of every hue were mixed in with an assortment of trees, shrubs, and bird houses. The proud owners took anyone who stopped by on a tour. ✳ Another of our favorite pleasures is the garden tour. There are so many to choose from, especially in June when gardens are at their lushest. To see gardens not on the tours you need only know the right person, which could be the owner or the head gardner, the pool designer, the lighting engineer, or even the fence installer. There's more than one green thumb in every grand garden. We take any and all invitations to visit gardens. They're as varied as the houses, and the driveways are often so long you need a bike. Have you ever heard of house envy? Well, now there's garden envy!

SOME ARE FORMAL, PERFECTLY TRIMMED AND SHAPED, not a leaf out of place, and others are more Arcadian and romantic. No matter the style, each has its own charm and its own history. Always inspired on these tours, we make endless to-do lists for our own gardens—"add some of that lovely border plant along the walkway" or "look for this flowering vine at the nursery"—but by the time we get home we have enough ideas for the whole neighborhood!

The seasons mark the passage of time, and gardens are the embodiment of that inevitable change. Some people love gardens in winter when it's the bones, the naked structure of trees and shrubs, that are exposed, and the bare outline of deciduous trees is softened by evergreens. As for us, we love the wintertime because it is easier to peek through the privets and see the defining features of a garden. If you view a garden for the first time in winter, revisiting it in the summer can be an enlightening experience.

Gardens can conjure up all sorts of memories and images. A swing hanging from a branch of a hundred-year-old elm reminds us of our childhood swinging away, not a care in the world. Or the time as a youngster when you planted a seed or a young shoot and eagerly checked it every day, carefully monitoring each stage of growth—it made you feel like every finger was green, like you were responsible for this life blossoming in front of you.

Gardening is like decorating your house: some do it themselves and others hire a professional. We both designed our gardens to fit the setting. Whoever it was that said, "A green thumb is a dirty thumb," had it right, because getting dirty is half the fun of it. Few activities bring such stimulation to the senses: You see it, you smell it, you touch it, and you can even hear it if you pay close attention. It has a distinctive hum, a chorus of industrious bees and wriggling worms and chatting birds, all going about the daily routine of living. Weeds drive one of our friends so crazy she has a pillow that's embroidered with "The philosopher who said, 'A job well done never needs doing over' never weeded a garden!" Weeding the garden is for her like eating M&Ms—once you start, you can't stop!

Whether your garden is a tiny patch in the front yard or spread across acres and acres of land, it can bring the same level of satisfaction, accomplishment, and beauty into your life. Having a garden (and exploring others!) is one of our greatest pleasures in the Hamptons.

ON ONE OF OUR COUNTLESS PHOTO TRIPS THROUGH THE COUNTRYSIDE, we hide our bikes behind the dunes and cross over a narrow beach path, leaving behind the greenest field of waist-high corn and approaching the bluest ocean we've ever seen. Our husbands and friends meet up with us, and everyone relaxes, reads, or naps. It doesn't get any better than this. The conversation revolves around the scenery. The big sky seems endless, the ocean calm, and the edges of the surf sparkle as it rolls in and out. At the horizon, where sea and sky meet, you can actually see the curve of the earth. Although we have all brought something to read, it becomes impossible to focus, as we each contemplate the sight before us. The whole scene gives new

no better than this

meaning to the phrase "the sky's the limit," for here in this environment you feel there are no boundaries, no limits to the imagination. At one point there is absolute silence except for the sounds of the surf and the breeze coming off the ocean. ✶ But the salt air has a way of making you ravenous, and we have all brought something to contribute to this impromptu picnic: fried chicken, corn salad, several types and colors of tomatoes, watermelon, and chocolate chip cookies. And it never fails: everything tastes better at the beach. We decide to stay as day blends into night, snacking on the leftovers, and we lay motionless and silent not wanting to disturb the moment as we gaze up at the stars carpeting the deep-purple night sky.

Town Line Beach, Sagaponack

Gibson Beach, Sagaponack

Flying Point Beach, Water Mill

WHEN THE WINTERS ARE MILD being here is a delight. The roads are empty, and the hectic pace of summer has slowed to a crawl. The air is crisp, the stars are bright, and when the moon is full its light reflects off the ocean and night could pass for day. It is the best time of the year for a brisk walk on the beach.

PEOPLE USED TO SPEAK OF "SOUTH OF THE HIGHWAY" (Montauk Highway) as the correct address. It had snob appeal, and that was where everyone wanted to be. This is no longer true. The right address is not important today. People are looking for the extraordinary—that view of sea meeting land, being able to swim from your own sandy beach (or your neighbor's), a place to moor your boat, acres of space around you, the highest hill overlooking all of this—and they'll go anywhere to find it. Privacy and the space that enables it has become a precious commodity out in the Hamptons. ✳ But finding a place for summer pleasures and getting away from it all doesn't have to be about largesse. The size of the house, the number of rooms, the number of acres—none of these statistics matters. Whether it's a cabin, cottage, or castle filled with flea market finds or fine antiques, what's important is finding your own special place and filling it with familiar things to make it feel like home. Things that make you happy, that make you feel content. We know a couple who sends their guests down to the beach to gather rocks or shells on which the guests inscribe their names. Their inscriptions wind up on the mantle as mementos of their visit. ✳ Everyone talks about the houses in the Hamptons. For traditionalists there is the centuries-old farm house, Shaker-like in its simplicity, defying storms, salty sea air, and sun. Midcentury modernists have their pick of architect-designed houses and builder copies. In a continuing cycle, everything old becomes new again, so if your favorite look isn't in fashion, chances are it will be soon. Modernism bloomed in the 1950s and turned nightmarish in the 1980s when every builder and self-styled architect tried to recreate those midcentury boxes. The original structures on which those '80s houses were based are now highly coveted and extremely valuable. These jewels are precious few today as so many have been wiped out by the brutal Nor'easters that occasionally hit the East End.

home sweet home

Town Line Beach, Sagaponack

ARCHITECTS THESE DAYS ARE DESIGNING, ONCE AGAIN, the shingled summer cottage with gambrel roofs, many-paned windows, multiple fireplaces, and several out buildings—separate garage, pool house, guest house, potting/tool shed, garden house, and the must-have, an artist's studio—together creating a self-contained compound. Follies such as a treehouse or a child's playhouse are fun, too, lending interest and amusement. These new mansion-sized cottages somehow still manage to impart a feeling of hearth, home, and comfort.

The character of many houses is a reflection of the changes from town to hamlet. The Victorian shingled houses lining village streets are fronted with deep covered porches and rocking chairs swaying in the breeze. Some of the turn-of-the-20th-century houses are festooned with turrets, shutters, dormers, and columns, harkening back to the days of no air conditioning, wainscoted porch ceilings painted robin's-egg blue, and porches filled with wicker furniture that withstands the swelling caused by summer's humidity. Long driveways of crushed stone with a median of grass down the middle run past the house to a garage tucked neatly in the back, and occasionally you'll find a classic pick-up truck or a 1950s two-tone, long-finned Chevy convertible parked there waiting to be taken out for a Sunday drive.

Outside of town, farmhouses shield from view silos and huge sliding-door barns. Tractors are well-oiled and shiny, ready to go to work. It is not uncommon to arrive at the local general store to buy coffee and a fresh baked muffin and find not only your next-door neighbor who just finished building his weekend retreat, but also the local farmer taking a break after clearing his fields.

Unfortunately, only five of the original forty working farms exist today. The sobering tax laws and the rapid rise in the value of real estate over the last twenty years or so have radically transformed the landscape from what was once a prosperous farming community. But a major shift in the farming that still goes on has occurred. There's a new crop in town: Fields of potatoes and corn have been replaced by rows and rows of chardonnay and pinot noir grapes. The same combination of factors that helped grow delicious potatoes—sun, salty air, rich soil—now produces award-winning wines at such vineyards as Channing Daughters and Wolfer Estate Vineyards.

Sagaponack

Sagaponack

endnote

WE SIT ON THE PORCH AT ELLEN'S HOUSE WRITING REAMS OF NOTES for this book, which end up in piles on the brick floor. The farmer next door has just revved up his tractor— the sound is music to our ears. We pause to gaze across the field behind the house to the cottages along the ridge, which leads to the dunes and then to the beach. It's hard to stay focused. Pheasants dance across the field in a straight line looking like the Rockettes. A rabbit by the hedge decides this is home. We can hear the surf rumbling, smell the ocean spray in the air, and the sun is high and there isn't a cloud in the sky. The pressures of our other lives are held at bay. It is hard to believe that this place really exists, but as we go back to our brainstorming we are reminded of how incredibly lucky we are to be here.

glossary of place names

AMAGANSETT In the Algonquin language, the area's name means "at the place of good fishing," i.e., offshore whale fishing. The first white settlers arrived in 1680. BRIDGEHAMPTON A bridge built by Ezekiel Sanford, across the northern edge of Sagg Pond, was part of the original road from Southampton to East Hampton. Bridgehampton was once called Feversham. GEORGICA According to William Wallace Tooker (1848–1917), author of *Long Island Indian Place Names,* Jeorgkee was an Indian who "went to sea to kill whales for Jacob Schillinger of East Hampton" and lived in the area near Georgica Pond. It is possible that the name could be a corruption of the English name Georgia. Originally a pond, it was opened to the ocean to create a brackish environment. Such an opening, called a seapoose (many spellings), means little river. It's a publicly owned pond, but in recent years, public access has been blocked by private owners. MONTAUK Montauk Point was called Fischers Hoek on a 1655 map drawn by Nicholas Vissacher of Amsterdam. An Indian deed refers to *Meuntacut,* or "high land," one of many variants. Tooker believed that the Indian word referred to a fort or fortified place—that is, a stockade created by the early Indians. Such a fort, still standing in 1662, was located on Fort Pond overlooking Fort Pond Bay. NORTH HAVEN Now a village, this near-island was once called Hog Neck until 1842 when several families agreed to change the name to one that would "sound better to modern ears." A bridge eventually linked North Haven with Sag Harbor. A ferry crosses to Shelter Island. SAGAPONACK An area east of Bridgehampton known as Sagg until 1889, as well as Sagg Pond and Sagg Swamp. Josiah Stanborough built the first house here in 1656. Tooker credits the origin of the name to *sagga,* an edible tuber eaten by the Indians. SAG HARBOR Early English settlers on the South Fork discovered that a mainstay of the Indian diet was a tuber that grew in abundance in low swampy areas.

This edible tuber has many names: groundnut, Indian potato, wild bean, bog potato. The original pilgrims ate them during their first precarious New England winter and botanists believe it to be one of the most important of wild foods and, had it not been for the potato, the groundnut would have been the first tuber to be cultivated. The Indians called the plant *sagga* and the word found its way into *Saggabon, Sagabonak, Sagg.* The harbor of Sagg evolved into Sag Harbor, which was also once known as Great Meadows. **SHELTER ISLAND** From the Indian word *Manhansack* or *Ahaquash* or *Awamock,* which means "an island sheltered by islands." Once called Farrett's Island for James Farrett who, in 1637, received the island from Earl Stirling. **SOUTHAMPTON** The Indian name was *Agawam*: "a place abounding with fish." Some sources suggest that most of the original New England colonists of 1640 had ancestral roots in Southampton, England, and named it after that place. Another source claims that it was named in honor of Henry Wriothesly, the Earl of Southampton in England who had been a director and treasurer of the Virginia Company, a well known and respected figure in the New World of the 17th century. **WAINSCOTT** According to Hooker, the name first referred to Wainscott Pond, and was not Indian in origin but from the ancient method of preparing *wainscot,* that is, oak timbers or boards, an early export from the region. One source claims that the mud bottom of the pond was used to season the logs from which wainscoting was made. Others believe the name was derived from an English town of the same name, and still others believe it has Indian origins. **WATER MILL** The original hamlet took its name from a watermill built in 1644 by Edward Howell. Mill Road was the name of the original road, now Montauk Highway, that ran eastward from the original (1640) settlement at Southampton to the mill.

The text in this glossary was excerpted from *South Fork Place Names: Some Informal Long Island History* by William Mulvihill, which was published in 1995 by The Brickiln Press in Sag Harbor, New York.

ACKNOWLEDGMENTS

So many have helped and supported us during the development
of this project and deserve our warmest, most heartfelt thanks.
We couldn't have done it without the following:

Ross Bleckner
Alan and Terry Blumenfeld
Nicholas Botta, architect
Nancy Brown
Larry and Jody Carlson
Peter Chervin
Chuck and Leslie Close
Laurin Copen
Michael and Nancy Davis
Carolyn Denning, our excellent tour guide
Stuart and Sharon Frankel
Ron Guttman and Irene Chen
Betsy Johnson
Anne Kavanaugh
Allen and Robin Kopelson
Christopher LaGuardia, landscape architect
Ken and Roz Landis
Harriet Love
Marders Nursery
Ari Meisel, who always keeps me laughing
Elliott Meisel, for superior navigation by air and by sea
Yvette Milavec for lending me a great lens
Michael and Susan Nash
Richard Cohen Rockwater
Jim Kutz Rockwater
Joy Schwartzman
Mark and Cassandra Seidenfeld
Marty and Susan Shulman
The Tarlow Family
Karen Trippi
Michael Trokel
Adriaan and Michelle Vanderknaap
Toby Weinberger, our good friend
Gary and Nina Wexler, for their friendship and "great taste"
Peri Wolfman and Charles Gold

We'd like also to thank our editor Andrea Danese for her clarity,
and for leading us in the right direction and keeping us focused;
Brankica Kovrlija, our "wonder woman" of design;
Eric Himmel for his enthusiastic endorsement of this,
our second book; and the late Paul Gottlieb for believing
in us and giving us our first chance.

To our friendship and to the ones we love:
Louis and Ari
and
Brian, Keith, Jena, Oliver, and Mack
— S.P.M. and E.H.

EDITOR: Andrea Danese
DESIGNER: Brankica Kovrlija
PRODUCTION MANAGER: Justine Keefe

LIBRARY OF CONGRESS CATALOGING-IN-PUBLICATION DATA

Meisel, Susan Pear
Hamptons pleasures / By Susan P. Meisel and Ellen Harris ; photography
by Susan P. Meisel.
p. cm.
Includes bibliographical references (p.) and index.
ISBN 0-8109-4332-8
1. Hamptons (N.Y.)—Description and travel. 2. Hamptons
(N.Y.)—Pictorial works. 3. Hamptons (N.Y.)—Social life and customs.
I. Harris, Ellen, 1946- II. Title.

F127.S9M455 2004
974.7'25—dc22
2003020932

PRINTED AND BOUND IN CHINA

10 9 8 7 6 5 4 3 2 1

HARRY N. ABRAMS, INC.
100 Fifth Avenue
New York, N.Y. 10011
www.abramsbooks.com

Abrams is a subsidiary of
LA MARTINIÈRE

Page 2: Shelter Island **Pages 4–5:** Montauk
Pages 8–9: Taken from a copy of an 1858 map of Suffolk County
by Whitlock's of New Haven, CT. All portions west of Wainscott and
Sag Harbor, including Shelter Island, were recreated by an illustrator
Pages 166–167: Wainscott